HOW TO GROW
BEANS, PEAS
ASPARAGUS, ARTICHOKES & OTHER SHOOTS

HOW TO GROW
BEANS, PEAS
ASPARAGUS, ARTICHOKES & OTHER SHOOTS

GROWING LEGUMES AND EDIBLE SHOOTS, INCLUDING CELERY, CELERIAC,
GLOBE ARTICHOKES AND SEAKALE, WITH MORE THAN 180 PHOTOGRAPHS

RICHARD BIRD

southwater

This edition is published by Southwater,
an imprint of Anness Publishing Ltd,
Hermes House, 88–89 Blackfriars Road, London
SE1 8HA; tel. 020 7401 2077;
fax 020 7633 9499
www.southwaterbooks.com;
www.annesspublishing.com

If you like the images in this book and would
like to investigate using them for publishing,
promotions or advertising, please visit our website
www.practicalpictures.com for more information.

UK agent: The Manning Partnership Ltd;
tel. 01225 478444; fax 01225 478440;
sales@manning-partnership.co.uk
UK distributor: Grantham Book Services Ltd;
tel. 01476 541080; fax 01476 541061;
orders@gbs.tbs-ltd.co.uk
North American agent/distributor: National
Book Network; tel. 301 459 3366;
fax 301 429 5746; www.nbnbooks.com
Australian agent/distributor: Pan Macmillan
Australia; tel. 1300 135 113; fax 1300 135 103;
customer.service@macmillan.com.au
New Zealand agent/distributor: David Bateman Ltd;
tel. (09) 415 7664; fax (09) 415 8892

Publisher: Joanna Lorenz
Managing Editor: Judith Simons
Project Editor: Felicity Forster
Editor: Lydia Darbyshire
Photographers: Jonathan Buckley,
    Amanda Heywood and Patrick McLeavey
Illustrator: Liz Pepperell
Designer: Michael Morey
Editorial Reader: Marija Duric Speare
Production Controller: Steve Lang

ETHICAL TRADING POLICY

Because of our ongoing ecological investment
programme, you, as our customer, can have the
pleasure and reassurance of knowing that a tree is
being cultivated on your behalf to naturally replace
the materials used to make the book you are
holding. For further information about this scheme,
go to www.annesspublishing.com/trees

Previously published as *Growing Shoots, Peas
and Beans*

Contents

Introduction

All gardeners who are interested in what they eat will already have considered the practicalities of growing their own vegetables. Mounting concerns about the residues of fungicides, pesticides, artificial fertilizers and other chemicals in and on our foods have been intensified by the use of genetically modified crops and the dawning realization that it is almost impossible to know exactly what it is that we are putting in our mouths.

Growing vegetables in our own gardens, on even a small scale, can help to redress the balance. When you eat vegetables that you have grown yourself from seed or from rootstocks and seedlings bought from a reputable supplier you know that they are free from all taint of chemical. Even if you choose not to grow organically, you can use the minimum of artificial pesticides and fertilizers and time their applications so that you do not eat anything that has been recently sprayed.

GROWING YOUR OWN

The pre-packaged produce we buy in supermarkets and large food stores may look appetizing and tempting, but how often the vegetables disappoint us when we taste them. Yet when these vegetables are fresh from the garden and cultivars have been selected for flavour instead of uniformity and shelf-life, they bring interest, colour, texture and taste to everyday dishes.

People are often deterred from growing vegetables, partly because it is so easy to buy a range of unusual crops in the supermarket and partly because vegetables have a reputation for requiring a lot of effort. Most gardeners, however, are perfectly happy to sow seeds of half-hardy annuals or to cut back and divide perennials or to spend hours walking up and down their lawn, cutting it, raking it, aerating it, fertilizing it and weeding it. Growing vegetables involves many of the same techniques, but rather than putting the dead plants on the compost heap at the end of the year, the vegetables are destined for the kitchen and dining table.

Shoot vegetables such as asparagus, seakale, rhubarb and globe artichokes are long-term additions to the garden, which do not even involve the annual chores of sowing seed and planting out. Established plants of asparagus and rhubarb, for example, will continue to crop for up to 20 years. In a small garden these plants are as likely to be found in the flower border as the vegetable plot. The graceful fronds of asparagus are a wonderful foil to herbaceous perennials, while seakale bears masses of white, honey-scented flowers. Even rhubarb is decorative, with its striking red stems, green leaves and, in summer, large

LEFT Asparagus plants produce beautiful, ferny foliage which is as attractive as the young shoots are delicious.

ABOVE Peas can be grown successfully in containers. It is important not to let the tub dry out, especially in hot weather.

ABOVE Broad (fava) beans are best eaten straight from the plant, but they can also be dried or frozen for future use.

COOKING

The shorter the period between harvesting and cooking, the better the flavour and the greater the nutritional content of all vegetables. Peas and beans, podded or topped and tailed, should be cooked briefly in lightly salted, boiling water. The young shoots of asparagus and seakale are usually boiled or steamed in special pans, which keep the shoots upright so that the thicker bases cook more thoroughly than the soft, tender tips. Celery stalks that are not eaten raw can be chopped for adding to those soups and casseroles in which their distinctive flavour plays such an important part. Celeriac, too, imparts its characteristic taste to many cooked dishes, and, like celery, it can be cooked and served as a vegetable in its own right. Rhubarb is widely used as a dessert, lightly cooked with sugar or honey as needed and served with cream.

clusters of small, cream-white flowers. The striking flower-heads of globe artichokes can be used in dried-flower arrangements if they are not eaten.

Peas and beans – legumes, as they are known – are among the easiest vegetables to grow and are ideal for gardeners with limited space. A few runner bean plants can be grown up garden canes, while some types of pea can be grown in containers. In an established plot, legumes play an important part in crop rotation, enriching and fixing nitrogen in the soil, which can, in the following year, be used for greedier plants, such as brassicas.

HARVESTING

All vegetables taste better when they are fresh, so plan your planting to ensure the best timing for harvesting the different crops. Sowing over several weeks in spring and including hardy plants,

such as broad (fava) beans, will provide a harvest over a long period from late spring onwards and ensure that you do not have a glut of any one vegetable. Celeriac, a hardy plant, can be left in the garden in mild areas so that individual roots can be lifted as they are needed. Celery too, although less hardy than celeriac, can be left in the ground until the first frosts.

To extend the season for harvesting rhubarb, it is possible to force the plant by covering the dormant crown with a forcing pot; in just a few weeks in early spring tender young stalks will be ready for cutting and cooking.

If globe artichokes are grown in the flower-bed, make sure they are placed behind some taller growing decorative plants because removing the unripened flower-heads to eat them will spoil their overall appearance.

BELOW The flavours of fresh asparagus and early peas combine perfectly.

types of
shoots,
peas and
beans

The plants described in this book range from those, such as seakale, of which there is only one named cultivar to those, such as peas and beans, of which there are, literally, dozens of cultivars offering an enormous range of size, shape and colour. All, however, will yield a worthwhile and delicious harvest for the kitchen. If space in the garden is limited, it can often be more rewarding to devote some space to unusual vegetables, such as globe artichokes, that are not widely available in supermarkets.

Asparagus *Asparagus officinalis*

This shoot vegetable was once the food of the wealthy, and if you didn't have your own garden, you couldn't eat asparagus. Nowadays it is much more widely available, but shoots cut straight from the garden and cooked immediately have an incomparable flavour. Asparagus is not only good to eat, but the decorative foliage has a wonderful filmy quality about it. In a potager or decorative kitchen garden the great plumes of finely cut foliage make a fine display.

The young, tender shoots are the part of the plant that is eaten. The shoots emerge from below ground in late spring and early summer. Once they get more than about 15–20cm/6–8in long they become tough skinned and rather chewy and are then best left. The remaining shoots will develop into tall foliage stems with inconspicuous flowers and, eventually from the female flowers, orange-red berries.

Asparagus grows wild throughout Europe and has been eaten and

VARIETIES

'Accell'
'Boonlim'
'Cito'
'Connover's Colossal'
'Franklim'
'Giant Mammoth'
'Hâtive d'Argenteuil'
'Limbras'
'Lucullus'
'Martha Washington'

possibly cultivated from at least the time of the ancient Greeks. It has long been grown in gardens, but the main disadvantage is that it takes up a lot of space. If you have a small garden but want to grow asparagus, try planting one or two crowns in a flower border, picking the spikes in early summer and leaving them in the border as decorative foliage plants.

One of the attractive features of creating an asparagus bed is that it lasts for at least 20 years and, apart from a little maintenance, not much effort is required to produce a wonderful feast each year.

Asparagus plants are either male or female. Male plants have the advantage of being more productive and not producing seed, which readily self-sows. Asparagus can be raised from seed, but if you use your own collected seed the results can be disappointing; it is better to buy named varieties from a reputable supplier. An increasing number of F1 hybrids is available, and these produce reliable all-male plants.

Asparagus provides vitamins A, B2 and C and is also a good source of potassium, iron and calcium. It is a well-known diuretic.

PREPARING ASPARAGUS

1 Cut off the tough, woody ends. Trim the spears so they are all about the same length.

2 If you like, remove the skin. Lay a spear flat and hold it just below the tip. With a vegetable peeler, shave off the skin, working lengthwise down the spear to the end of the stalk. Roll the spear to remove the skin from all sides.

asparagus

Celery *Apium graveolens*

An important vegetable for the kitchen, celery is used in many dishes, including basic recipes such as stocks and soups. Its culinary importance is not reflected in the garden, however. At one time no vegetable garden was complete without celery, but it is seen less often today, which may be partly because it is slightly difficult to grow and partly because it needs a constantly moist soil to do well.

Celery grows wild throughout Europe and Asia, and it is rather surprising to learn that it has entered cultivation only in relatively recent times. The vegetable was first cultivated in Italy as recently

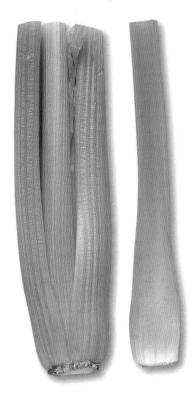

trench celery

as the 16th century, but it did not arrive in Britain until towards the end of the 17th century.

It is the blanched leaf stalks of celery that are eaten. These can be eaten green but will taste sweeter if the light has been excluded, causing the stalks to turn white. This always used to be done by heaping up earth around them, but more often these days the stems are wrapped in cardboard or felt. This type of celery is often referred to as trench celery. Hybridizers have developed celery with self-blanching stems, although not everybody agrees and many gardeners think that the old-style, blanched stalks have a better flavour. There are also cultivars with green, pink or red stems. There is a form of celery, known as green celery or American green, which does not require blanching.

PREPARING CELERY

1 Separate the stalks. Scrub them with a vegetable brush under cold running water. Trim off the root end, leaves and any blemishes (keep the leaves for the stockpot or soup). If the stalks have tough strings, remove these with a vegetable peeler.

2 Cut celery sticks into evenly sized slices as required.

Celery can be cooked or eaten raw. As well as the stems, some people like to eat the heart, the solid part of the plant, where the stems join the root. Some recipes also call for the leaves to be included, particularly when the celery is a flavouring agent rather than a vegetable in its own right. As well as being used to flavour dishes, the leaves can be used for garnishing – they have a more delicate flavour than the stalks.

Celery is very low in calories but contains potassium and iron.

Celeriac *Apium graveolens* var. *rapaceum*

Although it is often thought of as a root crop, celeriac (celery root) is properly regarded as a shoot, partly because it fits more neatly beside celery and partly because it is not, in fact, the root but the swollen stem that forms the vegetable. Like cultivated celery, celeriac is derived from wild celery, which is a native plant found in Europe and the Middle East. It was a much later development than celery, however, and is said to have been introduced to Britain from Alexandria in the early 18th century.

Because celeriac is the swollen area of the plant where the leaf stalks join the root, it is a hard, round vegetable, often with knobbles and leaf scars covering its dirty-looking surface. Although it looks far from appetizing, it is a useful vegetable. It is most frequently used as a flavouring, making an excellent winter substitute for celery, but it is also used as a vegetable in its own right, either cooked or grated raw in a salad. The leaves are too bitter to eat raw.

Celeriac is easier to grow than celery because it does not need blanching and is less prone to pests and diseases. However, like celery, it does need a reliably moist soil in order to keep growing. It should be given a long growing season or it will not develop into a size that is worth harvesting and eating. This means that you will have to start off the celeriac plants under glass.

Celeriac is low in calories, and is a source of vitamin C, potassium and phosphorus.

celeriac
(celery root)

BAKING CELERIAC

1 Peel the celeriac, then use a sharp knife to make 5mm/¼in slices, immediately plunging them into a pan of cold water acidulated with a little lemon juice.

2 Bring the water to the boil and simmer the celeriac for 10–12 minutes until just tender. Drain and arrange the slices in a shallow dish.

3 Pour a cheese sauce over the celeriac and bake in a moderate oven for 15–20 minutes until the top is golden brown.

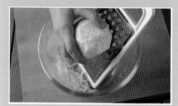

Celeriac can also be grated into a bowl, for adding to baked dishes.

Globe artichokes *Cynara cardunculus* Scolymus Group

Globe artichokes were not much grown by country gardeners in the past. They tended to concentrate on producing staple foods rather than on fancy and luxurious ones, and globe artichokes were regarded as belonging on the tables of the rich.

Globe artichokes are native to countries bordering the Mediterranean, and they are believed to be one of the earliest cultivated vegetables. They were grown by the ancient Greeks and Romans before spreading north into the rest of Europe. They are large, handsome perennials, resembling the cardoon (*Cynara cardunculus*), to which they are closely related. They are usually grown in the vegetable garden because several plants are needed to give a

BELOW Baby globe artichokes are mature artichokes that grow nearer the ground.

globe artichokes

constant supply throughout the summer, but if you have limited space in the vegetable plot you could easily grow a couple of plants towards the back of a large flower border. In the right conditions they will grow to 2m/6ft high, with a spread of about 1.2m/4ft.

There are several named varieties, of which the hardy 'Green Globe' is one of the most widely

available, producing large heads to 10cm/4in across. The similar 'Purple Globe' has decorative, purple-tinged flower-heads, and 'Gros Vert de Lâon' has flower-heads with an excellent flavour but is not reliably hardy.

Unlike most vegetables, it is the flower-head – or, rather, the bud before the flower begins to open – that is eaten.

Boiled and steamed globe artichokes contain some vitamin C, folic acid and magnesium and small amounts of protein and carbohydrate.

PREPARING GLOBE ARTICHOKES

1 Hold the top of the artichoke firmly and use a sharp knife to remove the stalk and trim the base so that the artichoke sits flat.

2 Using a sharp knife or scissors, trim off and discard the spiky top of each of the bracts and cut off the pointed top.

Rhubarb *Rheum* x *hybridum*

Gardening has many contradictions and rhubarb is one of them. It is a vegetable, but it is mainly used as a fruit – that is, it is eaten with sugar as a dessert. Tomatoes, on the other hand, are, strictly speaking, fruit but are used as a vegetable. Does it matter? These distinctions become problems only when you start classifying plants or writing books; in the garden and kitchen they don't matter at all.

Originally rhubarb was grown as a medicinal plant (the root was powdered and used as a laxative), and it was only much later that it came to be used as a vegetable. Forcing to obtain an early crop

rhubarb with leaves attached

was not discovered until the 19th century, less than 200 years ago.

Only the young stalks are eaten, and these must be cooked. The leaves are poisonous, so do not be tempted to experiment with them in an attempt to invent new dishes. The crop is normally harvested from spring to early summer, but it is possible to force it, by covering the dormant crown with a box, bucket or, if you can afford it, a decorative terracotta rhubarb forcer. This produces a crop of sweet-tasting stems several weeks earlier than if the plant is left uncovered in the open.

Rhubarb is an easy crop to grow and, once planted, it is not at all demanding. It can be left where it is for 20 years or more, although some gardeners prefer to replace their plants every five years or so in order to keep them vigorous. Rhubarb does

take up quite a bit of space, but a couple of plants will keep a small family well supplied. The space may be considered well used because rhubarb plants are also quite decorative in their own right, with huge green leaves and attractive red stems.

Rhubarb is low in fat, high in fibre, and contains good amounts of vitamin A and potassium. It is also a good source of calcium. Due to its tart flavour, however, it needs sweetening, which increases its calorie content.

PREPARING AND COOKING RHUBARB

1 Using a large knife, cut off and discard the leaves and the root end of the stalk. Peel off any stringy fibres with a swivel-blade vegetable peeler. Cut the rhubarb into evenly sized pieces.

2 Cook the rhubarb in a little water, with honey added to taste, for 15 minutes or until soft.

Seakale *Crambe maritima*

Seakale is one of the least widely grown and eaten vegetables, which is a shame, because it is not only easy to grow but is also delicious. Seakale has been in cultivation from at least the beginning of the 18th century, but the wild plant was harvested long before that. It is, in fact, native to Britain as well as to other countries of northern and western Europe, and to countries around the Black Sea.

It is a hardy perennial, and plants grow to 75cm/2½ft tall and 60cm/24in or more across. The large, fleshy, rather crinkled leaves are a distinctive blue-grey and are covered with a waxy coating to protect them from salt spray. From late spring to early summer clouds of small, white, sweetly scented flowers are borne on thick, sturdy stems. If space in the vegetable garden is limited, grow seakale towards the back of a flower-bed or border.

It is a member of the Cruciferae family, and, as with other brassicas, the leaves are likely to be eaten by the caterpillars of cabbage white butterflies, so affected plants can look rather untidy by the end of the season.

Seakale stems have a pleasant if slightly bitter flavour. Like celery, the stems are blanched before they can be eaten. Originally this was done by heaping shingle around the stems, but these days it is more likely to be done by covering the stems with a box or special

seakale

terracotta pot. The blanched stems are harvested in spring when they are about 20cm/8in long and boiled in the same way as asparagus – that is, by standing them upright in the pan so that the thicker

VARIETIES

'Angers'
'Lilywhite'

portion of the stem is cooked more thoroughly than the tip. The shoots are then served with butter, olive oil or a white or hollandaise sauce.

Plants are usually raised from root cuttings, known as thongs, from crowns, if they are available, or from seed, which can be sown in autumn or spring. It is a vegetable that varies little from its wild ancestor, and there are only a few named cultivars. One of the longest established is 'Lilywhite', a reliably heavy cropper, which has green leaves and well-flavoured shoots. It is, however, doubtful if all plants sold under that name are, in fact, true to the original cultivar. Because it is so difficult to obtain plants, it may be easier to grow from seed, discarding inferior plants and propagating from the better forms.

Seakale stalks contain some vitamin C and minimal amounts of sugar, fat and protein.

COOKING SEAKALE

Seakale can be eaten raw or cooked like asparagus. There is no need to peel seakale before cooking.

• To blanch, drop trimmed seakale stalks into a pan of boiling water and cook for 1 minute only. Using tongs, remove the seakale from the water and plunge it into cold water to prevent further cooking.

• To steam, place the seakale in a steamer insert and cook over 1cm/½in boiling water for 4–5 minutes.

• To grill, preheat the grill on high. Brush seakale stalks with a little oil and cook under a hot grill until bright green and tender crisp, about 2 minutes each side.

Peas *Pisum sativum*

Of all vegetables, peas are perhaps the best reason for growing one's own: it is impossible to buy peas that taste anything like those that are picked straight from the garden. However, the difficulty is that if you want to grow a succession of crops to give you peas throughout the summer, you will have to devote quite a large area to them. This is not the problem it once was, however, because the majority of peas are now much shorter, and even if you have space to grow only a few in a large bucket, the effort is worth it for the taste alone.

Peas are one of the oldest cultivated vegetables. They have been found in settlements from the late Stone Age onwards – that is, nearly 8,000 years ago. One of the advantages of peas is that not only can they be eaten fresh, raw or cooked, but they can also be dried and stored for later use.

Until about 50 years ago, peas grew to 1.8m/6ft or more and had to be supported with pea-sticks. Modern varieties are generally quite short, however, and can be easily supported with low wire netting or even a couple of strings stretched horizontally. Some varieties need no support at all.

There are several types of pea. First earlies are the earliest of the year. Those that are overwintered have smooth skins, but there are less hardy varieties, planted in early spring, which have wrinkled skins. Although they are less hardy, they taste sweeter. Second earlies and maincrop have wrinkled skins.

Mangetouts (snow peas), also known as sugar peas, can be eaten whole when the peas are still immature. Snap peas also have edible pods but can be eaten when they are more mature. Asparagus peas have winged pods and an asparagus-like taste. Petits pois (baby peas) are small, sweet-tasting peas.

Peas are a fairly good source of vitamins A, B3 and C, as well as iron.

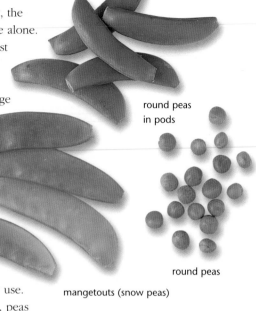

round peas in pods

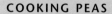

round peas

mangetouts (snow peas)

COOKING PEAS

To steam, cook, covered in a steamer over boiling water until tender. To boil, drop into boiling salted water, then simmer until just tender: 5–10 minutes for shelled peas, 1–2 minutes for mangetouts (snow peas).

Runner beans *Phaseolus coccineus*

Although many gardeners have given up growing peas because they take up too much space, few seem to have given up runner beans for the same reason, possibly because they are seen as better value for money and space because they continue to crop over a long period and it is possible to freeze any excess. As with peas, fresh runner beans are far better than those you buy in the shops, so the effort is certainly worthwhile.

Runner beans originated in Mexico, where they have been grown for more than 2,000 years, long before the Spanish conquistadors arrived. They were introduced to Europe in the 16th century but were at first grown more for their decorative qualities than for their culinary ones.

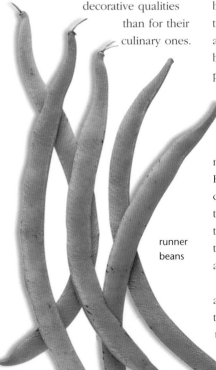

runner beans

Runner beans usually grow up to about 1.8m/6ft, although in good soil they will grow to 2.4m/8ft or more. There is, however, little to be gained from growing them so tall because it is difficult to harvest the topmost beans. Dwarf varieties are available for those who want them, but they have never become popular, partly because yields are lower and partly because all the beans tend to mature at the same time. The pods are long and rather coarse in texture, much coarser than the equivalent French (green) beans. This coarseness also applies to the texture, and it is important to pick the pods young – once they age they become stringy. Some varieties are less stringy than others.

The pods are usually eaten along with the young beans, but they can be allowed to mature and the fully grown beans dried and eaten later in the year, or stored for sowing next spring.

The general colour of the flowers is red, hence the old name of scarlet runner beans, but there are now other colours, including white and mauve. These are very useful in decorative schemes, and they still produce a good crop.

Runner beans are high in fibre and low in cholesterol and fat. They are a good source of iron.

PREPARING RUNNER BEANS

To top and tail beans, gather them together in one hand and then slice away the top 5mm/¼in, then do the same at the other end. If necessary, pull off and discard any stringy bits.

French beans *Phaseolus vulgaris*

French (green) beans are among the oldest type of cultivated bean. They originated in Central and South America, where they were being grown at least 8,000 years ago. They did not reach Europe until the 16th century, when they were introduced by the returning Spanish. The English name "French beans" presumably derives from the fact that they were introduced into Britain from France.

There are several forms of French bean, the main distinction being between the dwarf and climbing varieties. Climbing varieties have become a popular alternative to runner beans, and this makes them seem to be a modern development, but they are the older of the two types, dwarf beans not having been widely grown until the 18th century.

French beans are eaten whole, while the seeds are immature, or grown on and the seeds dried and used as haricot (navy) beans. Some varieties dry better than others. Pods can be green, purple or yellow, and round or flat. The flat varieties are more succulent, and the flat ones often become rather stringy with age.

Like runner beans, French beans are frost tender and must be sown or planted out after the last frosts. They need warm soil in which to germinate and thrive. They mature more quickly than runner beans and so provide a valuable early crop. They also have a quite different flavour and bring welcome variety to the kitchen.

Dwarf varieties are still the most popular, especially as they do not take up much room and are useful in small gardens. In addition, the yield is high and the season for each sowing is relatively long.

French beans are a good source of carbohydrates. They are a moderate source of protein, dietary fibre, vitamin C and beta carotene. The beta carotene is converted to vitamin A in the body. French beans also contain small amounts of calcium.

VARIETIES

Dwarf beans
'Annabel' green, slim pods, stringless
'Canadian Wonder' green, flat pods
'Daisy' green, long pods, stringless
'Delinel' green, slim pods, stringless
'Golddukat' yellow waxpod, pencil pods
'Golden Sands' yellow waxpod, stringless
'Masai' green, very slim pods
'Mont d'Or' yellow waxpod
'Purple Queen' purple, round pods, stringless
'Purple Tepee' purple, round pods, stringless
'Radar' round pods, stringless
'Royalty' purple, stringless
'Sprite' green, round pods, stringless
'Tendergreen' green, pencil pods, stringless
'The Prince' green, flat pods, early

Haricot (navy) beans
'Brown Dutch'
'Chevrier Vert'
'Comtessa de Chambord'

Climbing beans
'Blue Lake' green, round pods, stringless, white seeded
'Hunter' flat pods, stringless
'Kentucky Blue' round pods
'Largo' round pods, stringless
'Mont d'Or' golden, slightly flat pods, near-black beans
'Veitch's Climbing' green, flat pods

purple-coloured French (green) beans

climbing French beans

yellow-coloured French beans

French beans

Broad beans *Vicia faba*

Unlike other forms of bean, broad (fava) beans can be an acquired taste; not everybody likes them. However, when they are cooked straight from the plant, home-grown beans have a flavour that is never found in bought ones, so if you have not enjoyed them in the past, grow some and try them again – you may be pleasantly surprised. These beans also have the advantage of being one of the first vegetables of the year to mature.

While the other two main forms of garden bean come from the Americas, the broad bean is native to the Old World, probably originating in the Near East. Like the pea, it has been grown since Neolithic times, and, also like the pea, it can be eaten fresh or it can be dried and stored, which is a valuable attribute that has been appreciated right up to the advent of the freezer.

Broad beans are categorized in various ways. Sometimes it is by length of pod. The long-pods have up to eight kidney-shaped beans in each pod; the Windsors, the short-podded form, on the other hand, have only half that number of seeds, each of which is rounded.

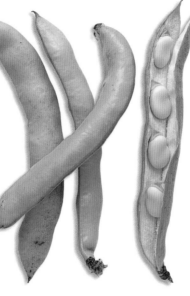

broad (fava) beans

They can also be categorized by the colour of the seeds (which range from pale green to mahogany) or by dwarf or tall forms (the former being better for the small garden). Finally, they can be divided into those that can be overwintered and those that are best sown in spring; this generally corresponds to the divisions between long-pods and Windsors, because the long-pods tend to be hardier.

Broad beans are low in fat and cholesterol, and are a good source of protein, iron, phosphorus and fibre.

ABOVE Broad (fava) beans are ready to be picked when the pods are round and plump and before the skin gets leathery.

VARIETIES

'Aquadulce Claudia' long-pod, white seeds
'Bunyards Exhibition' long-pod, white seeds
'Express' pale green seeds
'Hylon' long-pod, white seeds
'Imperial Green Longpod' green seeds
'Jade' long-pod, green
'Jubilee Hysor' white seeds
'Jumbo' large green seeds
'Masterpiece Green Longpod' green seeds
'Meteor Vroma' green seeds
'Red Epicure' red seeds
'Relon' long-pod, green seeds
'The Sutton' dwarf, pale green seeds
'White Windsor' white seeds

PREPARING BROAD BEANS

1 Cook broad (fava) beans in a pan of lightly salted boiling water for 3 minutes. Drain, refresh under cold water and drain again.

2 Remove the outer shells before adding them to salads.

planning and
preparation

As with all vegetables, shoots, peas and beans will do best when they are grown in soil that has been thoroughly prepared and that suits their individual requirements. This is especially true with long-term plants, such as asparagus and rhubarb. To give all these vegetables the best possible start and to ensure that they crop well, it is necessary to identify the type of soil in your garden and then to improve it through the regular addition of well-rotted compost or manure, through cultivation and through the removal of annual and perennial weeds.

Types of soil

Most shoots, peas and beans are deep-rooting and need a rich, fertile soil that contains plenty of organic matter. It is important that the soil does not dry out at any time during the growing season, so the soil must be moisture-retentive.

Identifying what type of soil you have in your garden is the first step towards providing the conditions they need. There are simple kits available for testing pH (acidity) and nutrient levels. To determine the structure, rub some moist soil between your fingers and try forming it into a ball. A clay soil holds together well and can be rolled into a sausage shape – heavier clay will roll more thinly, and can be smoothed to a shiny surface. Loam or silt will cohere but not press into shapes so easily. Sandy soil feels gritty and will not stick together.

CLAY SOIL

This type of soil can be difficult and heavy to work, and the particles cling together, making the soil sticky. Clay soil compacts easily, forming solid lumps that roots find hard to penetrate and making it difficult to dig. Try not to walk on clay soil when it is wet, which will compact the soil even more. In addition, clay soil is slow to drain in wet weather, but, when it is dry, it can set like concrete. It can also be cold and slow to warm up in spring, making it unsuitable for early crops. On the other hand, clay soil is slow to cool down in autumn, and it can be easily improved by the addition of well-rotted compost or manure and made easier to handle by the incorporation of grit. It is usually rich, and the hard work involved in the initial stages of improving it will pay off in the long term.

pH VALUES	
1.0	extremely acid
4.0	maximum acidity tolerated by most plants
5.5	maximum acidity for reasonable vegetables
6.0	maximum acidity for most fruit and vegetables
6.5	optimum for the best fruit and vegetables
7.0	neutral, maximum alkalinity for good fruit and vegetables
7.5	maximum alkalinity for reasonable vegetables
8.0	maximum tolerated by most plants
14.0	extremely alkaline

SANDY AND SILTY SOIL

Soils high in sand and silts are composed of large grains that allow water to pass through them quickly, and this speedy passage of water through the soil tends to

IMPROVING THE SOIL

1 Well-rotted manure will benefit all soil types. Spread it over the surface, and lightly dig in or leave for the worms to take it down.

2 Adding horticultural grit to clay soil will greatly improve the drainage and make it easier to work. Large quantities can be dug in when preparing a vegetable bed.

leach (wash) out nutrients, so that sandy soils are often rather poor as well as dry. However, they can be quick to warm up in spring, making them ideal for early crops. Silty soil contains particles that are more clay-like in texture than those found in sandy soils, and they hold more moisture and nutrients. Both types of soil are easy to work. Sand does not compact as clay does, although it is still not good practice to walk on beds, but silty soil is susceptible to the impact of feet. Adding well-rotted organic material will make both types more moisture-retentive.

LOAM

This type of soil is a combination of clay and sandy soils, with the best characteristics of both. It tends to be both free-draining and also moisture-retentive. This may seem contradictory, but it means that the soil is sufficiently free-draining to allow excess water to drain away easily, and waterlogging is unlikely to be a problem, but it is not too prone to drying out completely. This means that both water and air are freely available to the plants' roots, enabling them to take up the nutrients they need. Loamy soil is the ideal for which most gardeners strive.

ACID AND ALKALINE SOILS

Soils are also sometimes classified by their acidity or alkalinity. Those that are based on peat (peat moss) are acid; those that include chalk or limestone are alkaline. A scale of pH levels is used to indicate the degree of acidity or alkalinity. Neutral soil has a pH of 7; a pH lower than that indicates acidity, while a pH above 7 indicates an alkaline soil. Use a simple testing kit to check the soil in your garden. Take samples from several places, about 8cm/3in down – soil can vary within quite small areas – and follow the manufacturer's instructions.

TESTING THE SOIL FOR NUTRIENTS

1 Collect the soil sample 5–8cm/2–3in below the surface. Take a number of samples, but test each one separately.

2 With this kit, mix one part of soil with five parts of water. Shake well in a jar, then allow the water to settle.

3 Draw off the top few centimetres (about an inch) of the settled liquid, using the pipette supplied.

4 Carefully transfer the solution to the test chamber in the plastic container, once again using the pipette supplied.

5 Select a colour-coded capsule (one for each nutrient). Put the powder in the chamber, replace the cap and shake.

6 After a few minutes, compare the colour of the liquid with the shade panel of the container.

Improving the soil

Once you have established the type of soil in your garden, perhaps the most important tasks are to improve and maintain its quality. Good-quality soil is the aim of any gardener who wants to grow a range of vegetables, and to ignore the quality of the soil is to ignore one of a garden's greatest assets and will ultimately lead to poor yields.

IMPROVING SOIL QUALITY

The key to improving the soil in your garden is well-rotted organic material, especially garden compost, made from garden waste and vegetable waste from the kitchen, and farmyard manure. Both compost and manure are invaluable for improving the texture of the soil and also contain significant amounts of nutrients.

It is important that such material is well rotted. If it is still in the process of rotting down when it is applied to the soil it will extract nitrogen from the soil as it continues to break down. This is, of course, the opposite of what the gardener wants – the aim is to add nitrogen to the soil. A good indicator that the material has broken down is that it is odourless. Even horse manure is free from odour once it has rotted down. Some bought-in materials contain undesirable chemicals, but these will be removed if the material is stacked and allowed to weather. Bark and other shredded woody materials may contain resins, for example, while animal and bird manures may contain ammonia from urea. These chemicals will evaporate or be converted during weathering.

One of the great advantages of growing peas and beans is that they actually enrich the soil on which they are grown by fixing nitrogen in it, although this is possible only when the soil has a pH of 6.5–7. For this reason, in a crop rotation scheme legumes are usually followed by heavy feeders, such as brassicas, or by corn, which needs extra nitrogen.

DIGGING IN

When vegetables are grown in a dedicated part of the garden, the best way to apply organic material is to dig it in so that it is incorporated into the soil. If possible, double dig the bed, adding organic material all the way to the bottom of both spits. This will help the soil to conserve moisture and supply nutrients where they are needed, which is down around the roots. It will also encourage the roots to delve deeply, so that the plants are well anchored in the soil, rather than remaining on the surface where easy water can be obtained from rainfall and the watering can. The deeper the roots go, the more consistent will be the plant's water supply, and the plant will grow at a regular pace rather than in unproductive fits and starts. This will produce better plants and well-shaped vegetables.

TOP-DRESSING

Once the ground has been planted, it is best not to dig around the plants, because this is likely to

IMPROVING SOIL FERTILITY

The fertility of the soil is much improved by the addition of organic material, but a quick boost can also be achieved by adding an organic fertilizer, spreading it over the surface and then raking it in.

REDUCING SOIL ACIDITY

The acidity of the soil can be reduced by adding lime some weeks before planting, and working it in with a rake. Check the pH level with a soil-testing kit to see how much lime is required.

WORKING ON WET SOIL

It is best to avoid working on wet soil, but sometimes it is necessary. To ensure that the soil is not compacted and its structure destroyed, it is advisable to stand on a plank of wood while you work.

damage their roots. Organic matter can still be added, however, simply by spreading it on the surface of the soil around the plants. A layer 10cm/4in deep will be slowly worked into the soil by earthworms and other soil dwellers, and the dressing will also act as a mulch, protecting the ground from drying out as well as preventing weed seeds from germinating. Make sure that the top-dressing is free from weed seeds, or this last benefit will be lost, but hoeing off any weeds as they appear should not be too difficult. When garden soil has been thoroughly dug and plenty of organic matter added at the depth of one or two spades, many gardeners prefer not to dig the soil again. Instead, they apply a deep annual mulch. Applying a loose mulch, such as chipped bark or cocoa shells, will help to keep down weeds and conserve moisture in the ground.

AMENDING THE SOIL'S PH

The optimum pH for each vegetable is indicated in the final section. If your soil has a pH below 5.5, which indicates acid conditions, you can adjust the pH upwards by adding lime to the soil. Ordinary lime (calcium carbonate) is the safest form to use. Quicklime (calcium oxide) is the strongest and most caustic, but it may cause damage and must be used with great care. Slaked lime (calcium hydroxide), which is quicklime with water added, is not as strong as quicklime and is easier to handle. Choose a windless day, wear protective clothing and follow the supplier's instructions about quantities. Do not try to overcompensate for an acid soil by adding more lime than is recommended as this may lead to nutrient deficiency. Do not add lime at the same time as manure

ADDING ORGANIC MATERIAL

1 One of the best ways to improve the structure of the soil is to add as much organic material as you can, preferably when the soil is being dug. For heavy soils this is best done in the autumn.

because this will release ammonia. Do not sow or plant in the ground for at least a month after liming the soil.

It is more difficult to reduce the pH levels of alkaline soils. The traditional method was to dig in peat (peat moss), but not only does it break down quickly and need to be continually replaced, the collection of peat is now regarded as environmentally unacceptable. In any case, most soils tend to be slightly acid because calcium is continually leached (washed) out by rainfall, and most organic manures tend to be slightly acid and will help to reduce pH levels. Leaf mould, especially when it is made from pine needles, is also acid. If the soil in your garden is too alkaline for cultivating the vegetables you want, consider using raised beds, which you can fill with topsoil brought in from elsewhere.

2 If the soil has already been dug, well-rotted organic material can be worked into the surface of the soil with a fork. The worms will complete the task of working it into the soil.

Compost

This is a valuable material for any garden, but it is especially useful in the vegetable garden. It is completely free, apart from any capital required in installing compost bins, and these should last for many years, so the overall cost should be negligible. A little effort is required, but this is a small price to pay for the resulting gold dust.

THE PRINCIPLE

In making compost, gardeners emulate the natural process in which a plant takes nutrients from the soil, dies and then rots, so the nutrients return to the ground. In the garden, waste plant material is collected, piled in a heap and allowed to rot down before being returned to the soil as crumbly, sweet-smelling, fibrous material.

Because it is kept in a heap, the rotting material generates heat, which encourages it to break down more quickly. The heat also helps to kill pests and diseases, as well as any weed seeds in the compost. The balance of air and moisture is important; if the heap is too wet it will go slimy, but if it is too dry it will not decompose. The best balance is achieved by having some ventilation, by protecting the compost from rain and by using a good mixture of different materials.

The process can take as little as three months if the heap is large enough; a small heap may take much longer, but will still produce good compost eventually, as long as a suitable mixture of materials has been used.

THE COMPOST BIN

Gardeners always seem to generate more garden waste than they ever thought possible and never to have enough compost space, so when planning your bins, make sure you have enough. The ideal is to have three: one that holds new waste, one that is in the process of breaking down, and a third that is ready for use.

Bins are traditionally made from wood (often scrap wood), and because these can be handmade to fit your space and the amount of material available, this is still the best option. Sheet materials, such as corrugated iron, can also be used. Most ready-made bins are made of reinforced black or green plastic, and although these work perfectly well, they may be a bit on the small side in a busy garden.

ABOVE A range of organic materials can be used, but avoid cooked kitchen waste or any weeds that have seed in them. Clockwise from top left: kitchen waste, weeds, shreddings and grass clippings.

You can make compost in a bin the size of a dustbin (trash can), but if you have room in your garden, one holding a cubic metre/ 35 cubic feet, or even bigger, will be much more efficient.

MAKING COMPOST

1 To make garden compost, place a layer of "browns" – straw, dry leaves and chipped wood are ideal – into the bin, to a depth of about 15cm/6in.

2 Begin a layer of "greens" – any green plant material, except perennial or seeding weeds. Fibrous or woody stems should be cut up small or shredded.

The simplest bin can be made by nailing together four wooden pallets to form a box. If the front is made so that the slats are slotted in to form the wall, they can be removed when the bin is emptied, making the job of removing the compost easier.

MATERIALS

Most garden plant waste can be used for composting, but do not include perennial weeds. Weed seeds will be killed if the compost heats up well, but it is safest not to include them. You could have a separate bin for anything that contains seeds because the compost can be used on permanent plantings such as trees. If the compost never comes to the surface, seeds will not germinate. Woody material, such as hedge clippings, should be shredded. Kitchen vegetable waste, such as peelings, can be used, but avoid cooked vegetables and do not include meat, which will attract rats and other vermin.

ABOVE Good compost is dark brown, crumbly and has a sweet, earthy smell, not a rotting one.

TECHNIQUE

Placing a few branches or twiggy material in the bottom of the bin will help to keep the contents aerated. Put in the material as it becomes available, but avoid building up deep layers of any one material, especially grass cuttings. Mix them with other materials.

To help keep the heap warm, cover it with an old carpet or sheet of plastic, weighed down with large stones or bricks. This also prevents rainwater from chilling the contents and swamping the air spaces. The lid should be kept on until the compost is needed.

Every so often add a layer of farmyard manure if you can get it, because it will provide extra nitrogen to speed things up. Failing this, you can buy special compost accelerators. It is not essential to add manure or an accelerator, however – it just means waiting a couple of months longer.

Air is important, and this usually percolates through the side of the bin, so leave a few gaps between the timbers. If you use old pallets, these are usually crudely made, with plenty of gaps. The colder material around the edges takes longer to break down, so turn the compost around every so often. This also loosens the pile and allows air to circulate, thereby encouraging decomposition.

3 Add greens until you have a layer 15cm/6in thick. Mix lawn clippings with other green waste to avoid the layer becoming slimy and airless.

4 Kitchen refuse, including fruit and vegetable waste and crushed eggshells, can be added, but not cooked or fatty foods. Cover the heap.

5 Turn the heap occasionally. The speed of composting will vary, but when ready, the compost should be brown, crumbly and sweet-smelling.

Soil fertility

You cannot go on taking things out of the soil without putting anything back. In nature plants return the nutrients they have taken from the soil when they die and decompose. In the garden the vegetables are removed, and the chain is broken. Adding compost and other organic materials helps to redress the balance, but if you are to grow high-yielding crops, you will need to add fertilizers as well.

WHAT PLANTS REQUIRE

The main foods required by plants are nitrogen (N), phosphorus (P) and potassium (K), with smaller quantities of magnesium (Mg), calcium (Ca) and sulphur (S). They also require small amounts of trace elements, including iron (Fe) and manganese (Mn).

Each of the main nutrients tends to be used by the plant for one specific function. Thus nitrogen is

ABOVE The best way of adding nutrients naturally to the soil is to rot down old plant material in a compost bin and return it to the soil.

ORGANIC FERTILIZERS

blood

bonemeal

seaweed meal

fish/blood/bone

concerned with plant growth and is used for promoting the rapid growth of the green parts of the plant. Phosphorus, usually in the form of phosphates, is used to stimulate good root growth as well as helping vegetables to develop and ripen, while potassium, in the form of potash, is used to promote flowering and the formation of good crops.

THE NATURAL WAY

The most natural way to add nutrients to the soil is to use compost and other organic matter. Such materials are important to the general structure of the soil, but

they also feed it. Adding well-rotted farmyard manure and garden compost has been the main way that gardeners have traditionally fed their gardens. However, some gardeners, especially those in towns, may not have easy access to large quantities of these organic materials, nor the space to store them. Concentrated fertilizers, either organic or inorganic, can be a quick and simple way of giving plants the nutrients they need.

Organic materials normally contain less of the main nutrients than concentrated fertilizers, but they are often strong in trace elements, and even though they may not contain such a high concentration of nitrogen, they do release it over a longer period, which is of great benefit to plants. Because of their other attributes, well-rotted farmyard manure and garden compost are still the best way of treating the soil and of improving its texture.

ORGANIC FERTILIZERS

Concentrated fertilizers can be either organic or inorganic. Organic fertilizers are made from naturally occurring organic materials. Bonemeal (ground-up bones) is quite strong in nitrogen and phosphates, making it a good fertilizer to promote growth, especially at the start of a plant's life. Bonemeal also has the advantage that it breaks down slowly, releasing the fertilizer over a long period. When you apply bonemeal, you may want to wear gloves. Other organic fertilizers include fish, blood and bone (containing quick-release nitrogen and also phosphorus); hoof and horn (high in nitrogen); and seaweed meal (containing nitrogen and potassium). Because they are purely natural products, they are used by organic growers.

INORGANIC FERTILIZERS

These are fertilizers that have been made artificially, although they are frequently derived from natural rocks and minerals and the process may just involve crushing. They are concentrated and are usually soluble in water. This means that they are instantly available for plants and are useful for giving a plant a push when it is required. They do tend to wash out of the soil and need to be replaced regularly. Some are general fertilizers, with equal proportions of nitrogen, phosphorus and potassium. Others are much more specific. Superphosphate, for example, is entirely used for supplying phosphorus; potash (potassium sulphate) provides potassium; and ammonium nitrate is added when nitrogen is required.

Increasing numbers of gardeners are turning against inorganic fertilizers, unaware that they may not be as artificial as is generally believed. Many are not classified as organic simply because they are not derived from living things. Nevertheless, it is their concentrated form and the fact that they can be readily washed from the soil that leads many gardeners to object to their use.

SLOW-RELEASE FERTILIZERS

A modern trend is to coat fertilizers so they are released slowly into the soil. These are expensive in the short term, but because they do not leach (wash) away and do not need to be replaced as frequently, they save trouble and ensure that there is a regular nutrient supply. They are particularly useful for containers, where constant watering is necessary (with its attendant rapid leaching away of nutrients).

INORGANIC FERTILIZERS

Growmore (not available in USA)

sulphate of ammonia

potash

superphosphate

Digging the soil

Although it is a technique that is now being questioned by some gardeners, digging is still one of the main garden activities. It breaks up the soil, allowing the ingress of water and air, which are both important for plant growth. In addition, it also allows organic material to be incorporated deep down in the soil, right where the roots need it.

Digging enables you to remove weed roots – especially important on previously uncultivated ground – and it also helps bring pests to the surface, where many will die or be eaten by birds or other predators.

SINGLE DIGGING

The most frequently carried out method is single digging, and there are two ways, one informal and the other formal. The informal method is best used when the ground is quite loose; the gardener simply forks over the soil, turning it and replacing it in the same position, hardly using any trench at all. This process is often carried out on light or sandy soils.

Formal single digging is necessary on heavier soils and when there is organic material to be incorporated. First, a trench is dug across the width of the plot, and the earth from the trench is taken to the other end of the bed. Compost or farmyard manure is put into the bottom of the trench and then another trench is dug. The earth removed from the second trench is put into the first trench

ABOVE After a winter exposed to the weather, most soils can be broken down into a fine tilth by using a rake. More recently turned soil may need to be broken down with a heavier hoe first.

SINGLE DIGGING

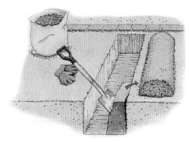

1 Start by digging a trench to one spade's depth across the plot, putting the soil from the first trench to one side to be used later in the final trench.

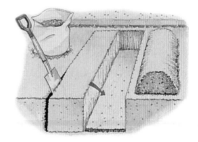

2 Put a layer of manure in the bottom of the trench. Dig out the next trench and cover the manure with earth taken from the second trench.

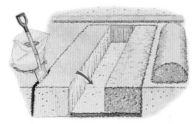

3 Repeat this process of adding manure to each trench and filling in with earth from the next, breaking up the soil as you go and keeping the surface even.

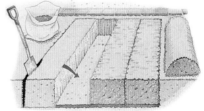

4 Continue down the length of the plot until you reach the final trench. This should be filled in with the earth taken from the first trench.

to cover the organic material. This procedure is repeated down the length of the plot. When the final trench has been dug and organic material placed in it, it is filled with the soil from the first trench.

Alternatively, the first trench can be dug so that it is two trenches wide. Organic material is put in the bottom as usual, and then the next trench is dug but the soil is spread over the bottom of the previous two trenches, only half-filling them. This is then covered with more organic material and the fourth trench is dug, filling up the first.

DOUBLE DIGGING

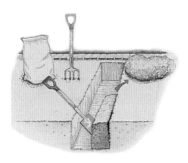

1 Dig a trench to one spade's depth, placing the soil to one side to be used later when filling in the final trench.

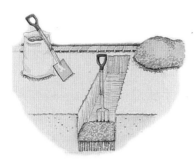

2 Break up the soil at the bottom of the trench, adding manure to the soil as you proceed.

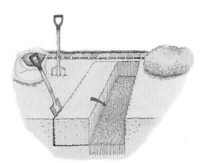

3 Dig the next trench, turning the soil over on top of the broken soil in the first trench.

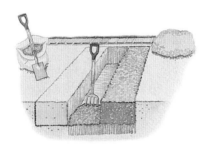

4 Continue down the plot, ensuring that subsoil from the bottom of the trenches is not mixed with topsoil.

Trenches three and four are treated in the same way, being filled first with the soil from trench five and then that from trench six.

DOUBLE DIGGING

Double digging is employed to break up the subsoil and is useful on any new plot of ground as well as when deep beds are being prepared. Dig the trench as before, taking the earth to the end of the plot. Break up the subsoil in the bottom of the trench to the depth of a fork or spade, adding in organic material. Add more organic material on top and then dig the next trench,

placing the soil into the first. Repeat until the end of the plot is reached. Do not bring any subsoil to the top.

MECHANICAL DIGGING

A mechanical rotavator (rototiller) can save time and effort on a large plot. One disadvantage is that it cuts up weed roots into small pieces, making them more difficult to remove by hand than with conventional digging.

RIGHT For larger gardens with heavy soil, a rotavator (rototiller) will break down the soil into a fine tilth. Even a small one saves a lot of time, especially if the soil is too dry to break down with a rake.

BREAKING DOWN INTO A FINE TILTH FOR SOWING

The best time to dig a heavy soil is in the autumn, then the winter frosts and rain will break it down for you. If clay soils are dug in the spring and allowed to dry out too much, they are difficult to break down because the clods set like concrete. A mechanical rotavator makes breaking the soil down easier. Work on the soil when it is neither waterlogged nor completely dry, breaking it down, first with a large hoe and then with a rake. Shuffling along the surface with your feet will also help considerably, but do not do this if the ground is wet.

It is better to leave sandy and silty soils until the spring because they do not need much breaking down. Raking the surface is usually all that is required.

Occasionally the soil becomes too hard to break down. If this happens, water the soil with a sprinkler, leave it to dry slightly – so that it is no longer muddy – and then break it down. Alternatively, draw out a deep sowing row in the rough soil, fill it with potting compost (soil mix) and sow in this.

Sowing in the open

In areas with short growing seasons the seed of peas, beans, celery and celeriac can be got off to a good start by sowing under glass. However, in milder areas peas and beans can be safely sown outside, and they will not then suffer the check to their growth that transplanting can cause. Asparagus seed is expensive and should be started under glass. Seed of globe artichokes, seakale and rhubarb is available, but these plants are usually grown from root cuttings, planted where they are to grow.

PREPARING THE SOIL

To give the seeds a good start, prepare the soil carefully. Several weeks before you plan to sow, remove any weeds that have appeared and rake the soil to break it down into a fine tilth. Cloches or movable frames can also be used to warm up the soil and to prevent it from getting too wet in spring downpours. A floating mulch, such as horticultural fleece or even sheets of newspaper, which can be held down with U-shaped lengths of wire or stones, will also help, but may be less effective than sheets of black plastic. The seeds can be sown in X-shaped cuts in the plastic, which can be left in place to act as a weed-suppressing mulch. Remember to water under a permanent mulch before planting. Fleece or woven types of plastic will allow rain through.

SELECTING SEED

Most of the seed that is available these days is of a high quality, especially when it comes from one of the major suppliers, and the rate of germination is usually good, although from time to time a batch may prove to be unsatisfactory. Non-germination is usually due to a factor such as planting into ground that is too wet or too cold, a particular problem with peas.

Many gardeners like to save their own seed, especially if they are growing unusual or heritage varieties. Bought seed, however, is usually of F1 hybrids, which means that the seed is of first-generation plants, obtained by crossing two selected parents. The plants growing from such seed will be vigorous, uniform and, in the case of vegetables, high yielding. They might also show resistance to particular pests and diseases. The seed collected from such plants, however, will not necessarily come true to type.

SOWING SEED

The conventional way of sowing seeds is in rows, which makes it easy to mark where they are, so that you won't accidentally hoe or walk on the emerging seedlings

LEFT Hoeing is the traditional way of keeping a vegetable garden free of weeds. A draw hoe or swan-neck hoe is pulled towards the gardener in a series of chopping movements.

1 Draw out a shallow drill with the corner of a draw hoe, using a garden line to ensure that it is straight.

2 If the soil is dry, water along the length of the drill and allow it to drain before sowing seed.

3 Sow seed individually or in threes at the recommended distances, or sprinkle thinly, depending on the vegetable.

4 Put a label at the end of the row clearly showing what is in the row Put a stick or another label at the far end. Do this before filling in the drill.

5 Rake the soil over to cover the seed at the recommended depth. Gently tamp down the soil with the flat of the rake and then lightly rake over

6 If the soil is heavy and is difficult to break into a fine tilth, draw out the drill and then line it with potting compost (soil mix) before sowing.

or pull them up while weeding. Use garden twine for guidance and a cane or length of wood so that you space the seeds appropriately.

If the ground is dry, water the planting hole before sowing the seed at the depth recommended on the packet. Peas and beans are generally sown individually where the plants are to be, rather than sprinkled along the row and thinned out later, since the germination rate is usually good and the seedlings dislike being disturbed. Most of the shoot vegetables, unless started under glass, are sprinkled thinly along the drill.

PROTECTING SEED

Speed of germination can be increased by protecting each group of seeds with a cloche which keeps the soil and seed warm. Remove the cloche, just during the daytime at first, once the seed has germinated, and protect the tender young seedlings from slugs.

Newly sown seed and freshly cultivated ground is always attractive to birds, which will enjoy using the fine soil for dust baths, and many will also eat the seeds or seedlings. Protect the seeds by erecting wire-netting guards, or leave the cloches in place until the

seedlings have grown large enough to withstand being pulled out by hungry birds.

LABELLING

Before covering the seed with soil, mark the end of the rows with pegs and a label. Once the drill is filled in, it is difficult to see where it is. It may be some time before the seedlings emerge, and the row can be easily disturbed by, for example, accidentally hoeing through it. Similarly, it is important to know exactly what you have sown, so the label should bear the name and variety of the vegetable.

Sowing under glass

Germinating seeds under glass is more tedious and time-consuming than sowing direct into the ground, but raising plants in this way has its advantages. It allows the gardener to grow reasonably sized plants that are ready to set out as soon as the weather allows, stealing a march on those sown in the soil by two or more weeks. If there are pest problems, such as slugs or birds, the plants are better able to resist them if they are well grown when they are planted out than if they have to fight for their life as soon as they emerge through the soil.

CONTAINERS

Seeds can be sown in a variety of containers. Traditionally they were sown in wooden trays or flats. Some gardeners prefer to make their own, claiming that they are warmer and that they can be made deeper than the purchased equivalents. Plastic trays have,

ABOVE A range of pots and trays is available for sowing seed. Clockwise from top left: individual cells, a half tray, plastic pots, a fibrous pot and fibrous modules.

however, generally replaced the wooden varieties. They can be made of rigid plastic for repeated use or thin, flimsy plastic, to be used only once before being thrown away. Often, however, only a few plants may be required, and it is rather wasteful to sow a whole or half tray. A 9cm/3½in pot is usually sufficient.

Gardeners are increasingly using modular or cellular trays, in which one or two seeds are sown in a small cell. If both germinate, one is removed and the remaining seedling is allowed to develop without having to be pricked out. This method has the advantage of reducing root disturbance.

Even less root disturbance occurs if the seeds are sown in biodegradable fibrous modules. As soon as the seedling is big enough to be planted out, both pot and plant are inserted into the ground, and the pot allows the roots to grow through its sides into the surrounding earth.

SOWING IN POTS

Fill the pot with a good seed compost (soil mix), tap it on the bench, water, and sow from one to three seeds in each pot, depending on the size.

SOWING IN BLOCKS

Fill the cellular block with compost and tap it on the table to firm it down. Water, then sow one or two seeds in each cell. Cover with a light dusting of compost.

SOWING IN TRAYS

1 Fill the seed tray with seed compost and tamp it down lightly to produce a level surface. Water thoroughly, allow to drain, then sow the seed thinly and evenly across the compost.

2 Cover with a thin layer of compost, lightly firm down, water carefully and label. Labelling is very important because the seedlings of many types of vegetable look the same.

WATERING IN

Water the trays or pots by standing them in a shallow tray or bowl of water so that the water comes about halfway up the container. Remove the tray or pot as soon as the surface of the compost begins to moisten, and allow to drain.

PROPAGATORS

Propagators are glass or transparent plastic boxes that help to keep the seed tray moist and in a warm atmosphere. Some models have cables in them so that the temperature can be controlled. Cheap alternatives can also be made simply by slipping the tray into a plastic bag and removing it when the seeds have germinated. Plastic jars can be cut down to fit over trays or pots.

USING A COLD FRAME

1 Once the trays or pots of pricked-out seedlings are ready to plant out, harden them off by placing in a cold frame which, to begin with, is opened a little wider each day but closed at night.

USING A PROPAGATOR

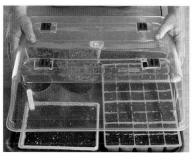

1 Place the containers in a propagator. You can adjust the temperature of heated propagators like this. Seed packets should indicate the best temperature, but you may need to compromise if different seeds need different temperatures.

HEAT

A source of heat is useful for the rapid germination of seeds. It can be provided in the form of a heated propagator, but most seeds will germinate in a warm greenhouse or even within the house.

SOWING SEED

Fill the seed tray with a good quality seed or potting compost (soil mix). Gently firm down and sow the seeds thinly on the surface.

2 Finally leave the lights of the cold frame off altogether so that the plants become accustomed to outside temperatures. Keep an eye on the weather and cover if frost is forecast.

2 This propagator is unheated and should be kept in a warm position in a greenhouse or within the house. Start opening the vents once the seeds have germinated so that they begin the hardening-off process.

Cover the seeds with a thin layer of potting compost and firm down lightly. Water by placing the seed tray in a shallow bowl of water. Once the surface of the compost shows signs of dampness, remove the tray, let it drain and place it in a propagator or plastic bag. A traditional alternative is to place a sheet of glass over the tray.

SUBSEQUENT TREATMENT

As soon as the seeds begin to germinate, let in air and, after a couple of days, remove the cover altogether. If you are using a propagator, turn off the heat, open the vents over a few days and then remove the tray. Once the seedlings are large enough to handle, prick them out into trays, pots or modules. Make sure they are well spaced and keep them watered.

Before planting the seedlings out, harden them off in a cold frame or by leaving them outside for gradually increasing periods of time each day.

Garden tools

spade

fork

To look in the average garden centre you would imagine that you need a tremendous battery of tools and equipment before you could ever consider gardening, but in fact you can start (and continue) gardening with relatively few tools and no equipment at all.

Tools are personal things, so one gardener may always use a spade for digging, no matter how soft the ground, whereas another would always use a fork, as long as the ground was not too heavy. The type of hoe for certain jobs is another subject on which gardeners hold widely different opinions.

BUYING TOOLS

It is not necessary to buy a vast armoury of tools when you first start gardening. Most jobs can be done with a small basic kit. When you are buying, always choose the best you can afford. Many of the cheaper tools are made of pressed steel, which soon becomes blunt with use, will often bend and may even break. Stainless steel is undoubtedly the best, but tools made of this tend to be expensive. Ordinary steel implements can be almost as good, especially if you keep them clean. Avoid tools that are made of aluminium. Trowels and hand forks especially are often made of aluminium, but they wear down and blunt quickly and are not good value for money.

SECOND-HAND

A good way to acquire a collection of tools is to buy them second-hand. As well as usually being cheaper than new ones, they are often made of much better steel than cheap, modern ones and still retain a keen edge, even after many years' use. Another potential advantage is that in the past gardening tools were made with a much greater variation in design and size. If you go to buy a modern spade, for example, you will probably find that the sizes in the shop are all the same – designed for the "average" gardener. Old tools come in all shapes and sizes, and if you find modern tools uncomfortable to use you are more likely to find an old one that is made just for you.

Not all old tools are good by any means, of course, but by keeping an eye out and buying only good-quality ones you will end up with tools that will more than see you through your gardening career and at a relatively modest price. Look out for them at car boot sales (garage sales) and in rural junk shops (second-hand stores). Avoid antique shops where such tools are sold at inflated prices to be hung as decorations on the wall rather than to be used.

CARE AND MAINTENANCE

Look after your tools. If you do this they will not only always be in tip-top working condition but should last a lifetime. Scrape all the mud and any vegetation off the tools as

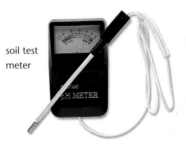

soil test meter

trowel

hand fork

gloves

Keep all blades sharp. Hang tools up if possible. Standing spades and hoes on the ground, especially if it is concrete, will blunt them over time. Keep them away from children.

EQUIPMENT

It is possible to run a vegetable garden with no mechanical aids at all. However, if you have grass paths a lawnmower will, obviously, be more than useful – it will be essential. Hedge cutters, too, are useful, although hedges can be cut by hand much more easily than grass paths.

In the vegetable garden itself the only mechanical device that you may require is a rotavator (rototiller), which can be used for digging and breaking up the soil. This is far from essential, even in a large garden – after all, some gardeners enjoy digging – but it does make life easier if you want to break down a large area of heavy soil into a fine tilth or if you are bringing some neglected ground under cultivation. Keep all your equipment maintained and serviced regularly, and always make sure you follow the manufacturer's safety instructions.

soon as you have used them. Once they are clean, run an oily rag lightly over the metal parts. The thin film of oil will stop the metal from corroding, and this not only makes the tools last longer but also makes them easier to use because less effort is needed to use a clean spade than one with a rough surface of rust.

In addition, keep the wooden parts of all tools clean, wiping them over with linseed oil if the wood becomes too dry.

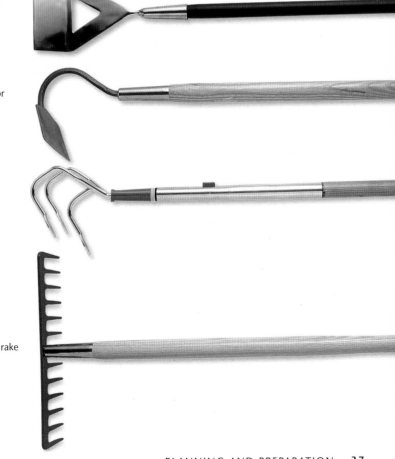

push, plate or Dutch hoe

draw hoe or swan-neck hoe

cultivator

rake

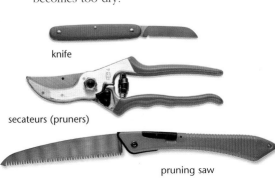

knife

secateurs (pruners)

pruning saw

Pests and diseases

If vegetables are planted in well-prepared ground, and fed, watered and weeded as necessary, they should grow strongly enough to be able to withstand most pest and disease attacks. However, in some seasons the problems may be too severe, and you may need to take action to control them.

SLUGS AND SNAILS

Most of the damage done to vegetables of all kinds in the garden is caused by slugs and snails, which will eat the above-ground parts of most plants. As a last resort, scatter pellets (metaldehyde or methiocarb), or spray with liquid metaldehyde. The poisoned creatures will harm birds that eat them, however, so it is best to control soil-dwelling slugs by using a biological control, nematodes, which can be watered into the soil in late summer. Alternatively, go out at night

BELOW AND BELOW RIGHT Snails can cause widespread damage and defoliation of plants. They can be caught in traps containing beer.

with a torch (flashlight) and collect all the slugs and snails you can see, putting them in a bucket of water so that you can dispose of them as and where you wish. Dishes of beer and upturned grapefruit skins can also be used to attract slugs, and some gardeners like to leave surplus seedlings near the vegetable plot so that slugs and snails will be attracted to the waste rather than to the crops themselves.

ABOVE Sticky traps are a form of organic control that is becoming popular for a wide range of pests. Here, pheromones attract insect pests to the trap, where they get stuck. Other sticky traps consist of sheets of yellow plastic covered with a non-drying glue. These are mainly used in greenhouses.

INSECT PESTS

The young shoots of most vegetables are infested with aphids from time to time. Remove small colonies by hand or with jets of

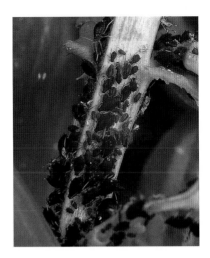

ABOVE Blackfly is a type of aphid that sucks the sap from broad (fava) beans, runner beans and French (green) beans. Natural predators usually control their numbers.

water. Encourage natural predators, such as ladybirds (ladybugs) and lacewings, into the garden by planting open, daisy-like flowers, such as poached-egg plants (*Limnanthes douglasii*) and marigolds. Blackfly can be deterred from attacking broad (fava) beans by removing the tender young tips of the plants.

Small black, yellow and red asparagus beetles appear in late spring or early summer. Pick them and the grey-brown grubs off by hand before they defoliate the stems, and clear away all debris so that they have no hiding-place to overwinter near the asparagus.

Celery and celeriac are related to carrots and are susceptible to carrot fly. A low enclosure of fine-mesh netting will protect plants from the low-flying insects. Digging over the soil in winter will expose any overwintering larvae to the birds. The leaves of plants affected by celery leaf miner or celery fly develop yellow blotches. Avoid the problem by growing the crop under a cover of fine mesh.

Pea and bean weevils, which eat notches from the leaves, will not harm strongly growing plants, and young plants can be protected with horticultural fleece until they are established.

Pea moth caterpillars eat all parts of the plant. Early- and late-maturing peas tend to be less susceptible, and flowering plants can be protected with horticultural fleece. As a last resort, spray with derris.

Pea thrips suck sap from both leaves and pods of peas and beans, causing discoloration and damaged, distorted pods. Early-sown crops tend to escape infestation.

DISEASES

Seakale is largely trouble free, but in wet, warm summers it is susceptible to the bacterial disease black rot, which causes the leaves to turn yellow. Like other brassicas, seakale can also suffer from club root, which causes the roots to become distorted and the leaves to be discoloured. In both cases, dig up and burn or throw away (don't compost) all infected plants.

A white, fluffy mould on globe artichokes, peas and beans indicates the presence of grey mould (botrytis), which is a common problem on many plants

RIGHT Grey mould (botrytis) affects peas and beans, but can be controlled by ensuring that plants are well spaced.

grown too close together. Remove all plant debris and make sure that plants are spaced so that air can circulate freely around them.

The serious, soil-borne, fungal disease violet root rot, which affects asparagus, celery and celeriac, is difficult to control, and if it is allowed to take hold it is better to abandon the bed altogether and replant the shoots in new soil using a batch of new, certified virus-free stock.

PHYSIOLOGICAL PROBLEMS

Celery and celeriac are prone to bolting – the production of flower stalks instead of edible leaf shoots. Make sure that the ground never dries out and do not allow seedlings to become potbound before planting out.

Boron deficiency sometimes affects celery and celeriac, and manganese deficiency sometimes affects peas. Check the mineral levels in your garden before planting and make sure that you add plenty of well-rotted compost or manure to keep the soil fertile and moisture-retentive.

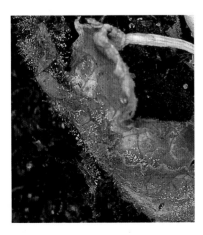

Growing organically

With increasing concern about the chemicals used in the commercial production of all vegetables and fruit, organically grown produce is rapidly gaining in popularity. Shoots, peas and beans are ideal crops to grow in an organic garden.

ORGANIC GARDENS

Organic gardeners aim to avoid using any artificial chemicals. This can mean tolerating a certain amount of pest damage – though there are a number of non-chemical control methods – but it allows predator populations to build up, so that in time a natural balance is established. Attracting the widest possible range of wildlife is the best way to achieve this – by growing a wide range of plants, putting out food and nest boxes for birds, and if possible by having a pond, which will greatly increase diversity. Companion planting can also reduce some pest attacks – for example, French marigolds (*Tagetes patula*) have been found to deter whitefly in the greenhouse, and some combinations of crops seem to have positive or negative effects on each other.

Rather than single or double digging the vegetable plot on a regular basis, organic gardeners often prefer the no-dig system. After an initial thorough digging to remove all perennial weed roots

and other debris, the soil is gradually built up by the annual addition of mulches of well-rotted compost and manure. Worms and soil-borne organisms take the nutrients down into the soil; the

gardener does not dig in the material. Because the ground is not disturbed by digging, the soil is not unnecessarily aerated (which increases the rate at which nutrients can leach out) and the natural

RIGHT Runner beans associate well with corn and summer savory but not with beetroot (beets) and kohl rabi.

layers of soil that develop over time are not destroyed. No-dig beds should not be walked on, as this will damage the soil structure, so they need to be accessible from permanent paths, and perhaps made as raised beds.

FERTILIZING THE SOIL

In addition to regular applications of well-rotted compost or manure, organic gardeners often sow green manures in ground that has become vacant. These plants are dug into the ground before they have set seed, to add organic matter. Many types, including alfalfa, beans and red clover, also "fix" nitrogen from the air into the soil, by means of bacteria in their root nodules.

One of the most useful and decorative green manures is the pretty hardy annual, the poached-egg plant (*Limnanthes douglasii*), which can be sown in autumn and will produce a good weed-suppressing ground cover of leaves, which can be dug in the following spring, before the flowers appear. This plant will set seed readily, and if it is allowed to grow on,, the flowers are useful for attracting beneficial hoverflies and bees to the garden.

The perennial Russian comfrey (*Symphytum* × *uplandicum*) is a vigorous plant that can be grown to produce a liquid feed. Once established, plants can be cut back several times a year. The nitrogen- and potassium-rich leaves can be added to the compost heap as an activator or allowed to rot in water to form a smelly but potash-rich feed. Although not as attractive as comfrey, the leaves of nettles (*Urtica dioica*) can also be used to make a good liquid feed, which contains magnesium, sulphur and iron. Young nettle leaves are also useful compost activators. But beware: both comfrey and nettles can be invasive.

BIOLOGICAL CONTROLS

There are a number of useful biological controls now available. In the open garden, a parasitic nematode, *Phasmarhabditis hermaphrodita*, can be watered into the ground to control slugs, but it can be applied only when the soil temperature is 5°C/40°F and above. There is also a bacterium, *Bacillus thuringiensis*, which can be sprayed on crops to kill certain caterpillars – seakale, for example, is often eaten by the caterpillars of the cabbage white butterfly. Some controls can be used only in the greenhouse, notably the parasitic wasp *Encarsia formosa*, which is very effective against whitefly, and a predatory mite, *Phytoseiulus persimilis*, which attacks red spider mite.

Biological controls usually work best when the weather is warm, and some are not suitable for indoor use. Introduce them as soon as the first signs of attack are noticed. Be patient and accept that there will be some damage before the biological agent takes effect. When you use biological controls there will always be some pests – they are essential for the predator to continue to breed – but the population will be reduced and any damage to your crops should be negligible.

ABOVE A "lacewing hotel" provides an area where lacewings – whose larvae eat large quantities of aphids – can live.

BENEFICIAL PREDATORS IN THE GARDEN

Frogs: These can be attracted to the garden by creating a pond. They are very helpful in controlling the slug population.
Hoverflies: Their larvae eat aphids. They can be encouraged into the garden by planting daisy-flowered or other open-flowered species.
Lacewings: The larvae eat practically all pests during their development. Attract them by erecting "lacewing hotels" in mid- to late summer.
Ladybirds (ladybugs): Eat aphids.
Tachinid flies: The larvae parasitize other insect hosts, especially caterpillars. They can be attracted in the same way as hoverflies.

cultivating
shoots, peas and beans

Most of the vegetables described in this book are not difficult to grow, and if some types present more of a challenge, it is that much more satisfying if you succeed. Whichever you choose to try, follow the cultivation techniques given here and you should be rewarded with a delicious supply of fresh vegetables throughout spring and summer, and even into early winter.

Growing asparagus

Asparagus needs an open, sunny site, and it likes a light, preferably sandy soil, although it can be grown in any soil as long as it is free-draining but moisture-retentive and reasonably fertile. In heavy soils it can be grown by raising the level of the soil or by making a raised bed. Asparagus prefers a soil pH of 6.5–7.5, so acid soil should be limed to raise the pH. In the autumn before planting dig the bed, removing all traces of perennial weeds and incorporating plenty of well-rotted manure or compost. In early spring dig out a trench 20cm/8in deep with an 8cm/3in ridge running down the centre. If more than one row is required, set the trenches 90cm/3ft apart. Set each asparagus crown on

CULTIVATION

Sowing
Sowing time: spring
Sowing depth: 1cm/½in
Distance between sown rows: 30cm/12in
Thinning distance: 15cm/6in
Transplanting: following spring

Planting
Planting time: early spring
Planting distance: 45cm/18in
Planting depth: initially 8–10cm/3–4in
Distance between planted rows: 90cm/3ft
Harvesting: in late spring for six weeks (third year onwards)

the ridge, spreading out its roots around it. Place the crowns 45cm/18in apart and cover them with soil to a depth of 8–10cm/3–4in.

If you are growing from seed, soak them overnight in water and sow in a drill 1cm/½in deep. Do this in spring. Thin to 15cm/6in and transplant the following spring in the same manner as for bought crowns above. As the plants grow, draw in more earth from the side of the trench until it is filled.

Do not cut any spears in the first year and only one or two from each plant during the next year. Each spring, cover the trench with a layer of manure or compost, leaving it slightly heaped up so that over the years the row becomes earthed (hilled) up, in the same way you treat potatoes. Keep the ground weeded. Cut down the ferns as they begin to turn yellow and, if possible, before the berries

APPLYING A SPRING MULCH

In the spring, before growth starts, apply a deep mulch of well-rotted manure over the rows of asparagus.

HARVESTING

Harvest asparagus by carefully cutting the stems below the ground. Use a sharp knife to make a clean, slanting cut about 5cm/2in deep in the ground. When cutting, take care that you do not damage the roots.

ABOVE Once the harvesting season is over, the asparagus can be left to grow to its full height.

begin to ripen; alternatively, pick all the berries. If they are left on the plants the birds will eat them and before long asparagus will be appearing all over the garden. For the same reason, avoid putting berried stems on the compost heap.

HARVESTING

In late spring, when the shoots that have emerged are 10–15cm/4–6in long, cut them by inserting a knife 5cm/2in below the surface of the soil. Only cut through the stem, do not thrash around below the soil level or you may damage spears that have not yet emerged. Make a slanting cut. After the third year cutting can take place over a period of about six weeks.

STORAGE

Asparagus is best used fresh from the plant, but it can be stored for a couple of days if it is stood in a jug of cold water in the refrigerator.

PESTS AND DISEASES

Slugs are likely to be the worst problem, making holes in the spears. Asparagus beetle can also be a nuisance. Violet rot can be a problem in an established bed of asparagus.

CUTTING DOWN IN AUTUMN

In the autumn, as the asparagus fronds are beginning to turn brown, cut them down to the ground.

Growing celery

Celery does best in fertile, moisture-retentive soil with a pH of 6.5–7.5. There are two ways of growing celery, depending on whether you are growing trench or self-blanching varieties. To grow traditional trench celery, in the preceding autumn or winter dig a trench 45cm/18in wide and 30cm/12in deep and put in an 8cm/3in layer of rotted manure. Backfill the trench, leaving it about 10cm/4in deep. Sow the seeds under glass in modules in early spring and place them in moderate heat of 10–16°C/50–61°F. Do not check the plants by subjecting them to a sudden change of temperature or by allowing them to dry out. Once the frosts are over, harden off the plants and plant them out in the trench at 30cm/12in intervals. When the plants reach about 30cm/12in, tie the stems loosely together just below the leaves and draw up earth over part of the

ABOVE Some varieties of celery, such as green or American celery, do not need blanching to make them sweet. Green celery is also more nutritious than blanched.

stems. Repeat the process three weeks later, pulling up more soil, and again three weeks after this, until the soil is up to the lower leaves. Alternatively, plant on flat ground and wrap cardboard, felt

CULTIVATION

Trench
Sowing time: early to mid-spring
Planting time: early summer
Planting distance: 30cm/12in
Distance between planted rows:
  60cm/24in
Harvesting: autumn

Self-blanching
Sowing time: early to mid-spring
Planting time: early summer
Planting distance: in blocks
  23cm/9in
Harvesting: autumn

or waterproof paper round the stems when they are 30cm/12in long. When the stems grow taller, wrap a second collar round them. Keep the celery well watered and do not allow the soil to dry out.

Self-blanching celery is started in the same way from seed and then planted out in blocks rather than rows, with the plants set out at intervals of 23cm/9in in all

BLANCHING

1 Blanching stems of trench celery will make them taste sweeter. When the stems reach a height of about 30cm/12in, tie them loosely together just below the leaves.

2 A collar of cardboard, felt or waterproof paper is tied around the stems of celery. The stems eventually blanch because of the lack of light, and they are not palatable unless this is done.

3 Soil can be used to hold the collar in place. Although soil can also be earthed up around the stems to blanch them, a collar will stop soil from getting into the crown.

directions. The dense foliage helps to blanch the stems. Place straw around the outside of the block to help keep out the light. Green celery can be grown in the same way, but there is no need for the straw.

HARVESTING

Trench celery can be lifted in autumn by digging it up with a fork. Replace soil around the next plant if it falls away. Continue to dig as required. The flavour is improved by the first frosts, but cover the plants with straw in severe weather so that penetrating frosts do not reach the stems. Self-blanching celery can also be harvested as required from the autumn onwards, but it should be lifted by the time of the first winter frosts.

STORAGE

Leave trench varieties where they are growing until required. In colder areas, before the weather becomes severe, lift and store in a frost-free place, where they should stay fresh for several weeks. Celery can be frozen, but it becomes mushy when it is defrosted, so it can be used only as flavouring or in cooked dishes.

PESTS AND DISEASES

Slugs are one of the worst enemies of celery, and it is important to cull them regularly by your preferred method. Other problems can include celery fly and carrot fly.

Diseases include celery heart rot, celery leaf spot and violet root rot. Boron deficiency may cause the stems to crack.

HARVESTING

Harvest the celery by digging beneath it with a fork and levering it out of the soil. Replace any soil around the next plant if it falls away so that it grows on.

BELOW Celery can be planted about 23cm/9in apart in blocks, in well-manured soil. The stalks will be ready for harvesting 4–5 months after planting.

Growing celeriac

Celeriac (celery root), whose close relationship with celery is revealed in its alternative names, celery root or turnip-rooted celery, prefers an open, sunny position, although it will tolerate a little light shade. It does best in soil with a pH of 6.5–7.5, so if your soil is very acid you should grow it in soil that has been limed during the previous season. The soil must also be rich in organic material, not only to provide a steady supply of nutrients but also to help to retain moisture around the roots.

Because plants need a long growing season, celeriac is best started off under glass in modules or fibre pots in late winter or early spring. Place them in a propagator set at about 15°C/59°F, although

CULTIVATION

Sowing time: late winter to
   mid-spring
Planting time: late spring to early
   summer
Planting distance: 30cm/12in
Distance between planted rows:
   30cm/12in
Harvesting: autumn onwards

seed will germinate at 10–19°C/50–66°F. Delay sowing until late spring if the greenhouse is unheated. Maintain an even temperature and keep them well watered so that the growth is not checked. Towards the end of spring, when plants are about 8cm/3in tall, harden them off and plant them out at 30cm/12in intervals in rows set 30cm/12in

apart. Set the plantlets out so that the base of the stem is level with the surface of the soil. Water thoroughly and mulch around plants to help retain moisture in the soil.

To prevent plants from bolting (which can also be a problem with celery), keep young plants in a constant temperature that does not fall below 12°C/54°F, avoid root disturbance by growing the seeds individually in modules and never let the soil around plants dry out. In addition, do not allow seedlings to become potbound before planting out, or the roots will never

BELOW A row of celeriac (celery root) with perfect spacing between plants, and leaves trimmed from the tops of the bulbs.

be able to take up sufficient moisture from the garden. Choose bolt-resistant cultivars, such as 'Prinz'.

Cut off any side shoots that appear and towards late summer remove a few of the lower leaves. This will allow more light to reach the base of the stems and encourage them to swell. In cold areas cover the plants with a dry mulch of bracken or straw to protect them from sharp frosts.

Celeriac and celery are occasionally affected by boron deficiency. This can occur on very free-draining ground, from which nutrients are rapidly leached, on soil that is naturally very alkaline or on soil that has been too heavily treated with lime, which then prevents plants from taking up the available boron in the soil. Affected plants have cracks on the outer surface of the leaf stalks while the

LETTING LIGHT IN

Remove a few of the lower leaves from the bulb to let the light on to the top. This should be done in late summer.

WEEDING

Keep the bed weed-free, but take care if you use a hoe, so as not to damage the roots of the celeriac.

inner stalk turns a red-brown. Adding plenty of well-rotted compost and manure to the ground at planting will help to make the soil more water-retentive. If you know that the soil in your garden is deficient in boron, which sometimes happens when the underlying rock is granite, treat the soil before planting by adding borax, in the form of sodium tetraborate, at the rate recommended on the packet, mixing it with horticultural sand to make even application easy.

HARVESTING
Celeriac needs a long growing season – allow 26 weeks from sowing to harvesting – and plants should be left in the ground for as long as possible to allow them to continue to grow. They are edible when they are about 8cm/3in across, although in good seasons

WATERING

So that its growth is not checked, it is necessary to water celeriac regularly to ensure that the soil never dries out.

they can get to 13cm/5in or more in diameter. Leave them in the ground and lift as needed.

STORAGE
In mild areas celeriac can be left in the ground over winter, protected with straw or bracken if necessary. If your garden is affected by penetrating frosts, lift the roots in early winter, trim them to remove the outer leaves and keep them in a frost-free but cool place in boxes of just-moist sand or peat substitute.

PESTS AND DISEASES
Although largely trouble free, celeriac is related to carrots and is susceptible to carrot fly. It is also sometimes affected by celery fly. Slugs and snails will eat young plants. Plants are sometimes affected by fungal leaf spot, and violet root rot is the most serious potential disease.

Growing globe artichokes

Globe artichokes need an open, sunny situation in soil that has a pH of 6.5–7.5, although they will tolerate slightly more acid or more alkaline conditions as long as the soil never becomes waterlogged. Because the plants are left in the ground for three or four years, the soil must be thoroughly prepared before planting. Dig over the ground, remove all perennial weeds, and incorporate plenty of organic material, such as well-rotted manure or garden compost, into the soil.

Globe artichokes are usually grown from offsets rather than from seed, which tends to produce variable results. If you cannot find a supplier of offsets, you could initially grow plants from seed and select the best ones from which you can propagate by division.

This can be done by cutting off the young, outer growth from the old plant with a sharp knife in spring. Each shoot should be growing strongly and have some roots attached. Plant these out immediately. Divisions can also be taken in autumn, when the offsets can be potted up and overwintered in a frost-free greenhouse or cold frame.

Seed can be sown in spring under glass in modules, or outdoors in rows 30cm/12in apart. Thin seedlings to 15cm/6in apart, and transplant the following spring,

BELOW A bed of globe artichokes with heads that are nearly ready for cutting.

at intervals of 75cm/30in, in rows set 90cm/3ft apart. If grown under glass, harden them off before planting out. In areas where the winter temperature does not fall below –8°C/18°F seed can be sown outdoors in autumn.

Plant offsets at the same spacings as for seedlings. Trim off about one-third of each leaf to reduce water loss while the plant is getting established. Water regularly, especially in dry spells, to ensure that plants never dry out.

Although globe artichokes are hardy perennials, in areas where the winter temperature falls below –15°C (5°F) protect the root by covering the crown with a thick layer of a dry mulch such as straw or bracken. Because older plants

are not as productive as younger ones, plants should be replaced every three or four years, and when they are grown in the vegetable garden you should aim to replace a third of your plants every year.

HARVESTING

Plants will produce edible flower-heads from the second year onwards. Remove them before they begin to open and while they are still green by using a sharp knife or secateurs (pruners) to cut through the stem about 2.5cm/1in below the head.

STORAGE

Globe artichokes are best eaten straight from the plant. You can freeze the heads, but the stem and choke must be removed first.

PESTS AND DISEASES

Globe artichokes are not troubled by many problems. Aphids, especially blackfly, can be a nuisance, and slugs and snails can eat the young shoots. Grey mould (botrytis) sometimes affects plants grown in overcrowded conditions. Petal blight, a fungal disease that is especially prevalent in wet summers, causes the heads to rot; cut off and burn any infected flower-heads.

CUTTING BACK

Cut down all stems to ground level when the plant dies back in the autumn. Replace plants after three or, at most, four years.

COVERING WITH STRAW

Cover the plant with a dry mulch of straw or bracken during autumn in colder areas.

Growing rhubarb

Rhubarb needs a sunny position, away from shade. The soil should be rich in organic material but it should also be reasonably free-draining. Rhubarb does best in acid soil, with a pH of 5–6, although it will tolerate more alkaline conditions if the soil is fertile. Because the site will be in use over a long period of time, take care in its preparation, removing all perennial weeds and digging deeply to incorporate as much well-rotted manure or compost as possible. In the past new plants were bare-rooted and

CULTIVATION

Seed
Sowing time: spring
Sowing depth: 2.5cm/1in
Distance between sown rows:
    30cm/12in
Thinning distance: 23cm/9in
Transplanting: following winter
Division
Planting time: winter or (if potted)
    spring or summer
Planting distance: 90cm/3ft
Distance between rows: 90cm/3ft
Harvesting: summer of second
    year onwards

were planted in winter, while dormant. This is also a good time to divide an existing plant to start a new one: dig up the old plant and remove an outer section that includes at least one bud. Plants purchased in pots can be planted in spring or even summer if they are well-watered. They should be spaced 90cm/3ft apart.

BELOW A bed of healthy looking rhubarb is an attractive sight. Remember that the handsome leaves are poisonous and should never be eaten.

RIGHT A decorative terracotta rhubarb
forcer for producing sweet early rhubarb.
A box or bucket can be used instead.

Rhubarb can also be grown
from seed, but this method takes
longer and the quality of the plant
cannot be guaranteed in the same
way as buying a named cultivar.
However, the seed can be sown in
2.5cm/1in drills and thinned to
23cm/9in once they have germinated. Plant out in their final
position, in the same way as for
dormant crowns, during the
following winter. Water well in dry
weather. Apply a mulch of well-
rotted, seed-free manure in autumn
and again in spring.

To force a rhubarb plant, cover
it with a large upturned bucket,
box or other similar container in
midwinter. Do not force the same
plant for two years running or it
will be weakened.

HARVESTING

Harvest by pulling on the sticks of
rhubarb so that they come out of their
"socket". Cut off the leaves and discard
on the compost heap.

HARVESTING

Rhubarb is harvested from spring
to early summer unless it has been
forced, when it can be pulled a few
weeks earlier. It is harvested by
pulling each stem vertically from
close to the base – it will come out
of its "socket". Cut off the leaves
and discard them on the compost
heap – they are poisonous and
must not be eaten.

STORAGE

Rhubarb is best cooked straight
from the garden. Otherwise it can
be stored by freezing or bottling.

PESTS AND DISEASES

There are a few pests and diseases
that trouble rhubarb, but you will
be unfortunate if you come across
them. Honey fungus and crown rot
are the most serious of these.

Growing seakale

Seakale needs an open, sunny position. The soil must be free-draining – sandy or gravelly soil is ideal – and if your soil is very heavy it may be necessary to create a raised bed. It will grow in a soil with a pH of 6.5–8. Incorporate well-rotted manure during the autumn digging. Plants can be grown from bought plants, from root cuttings or "thongs" or from seed. Bought plants should be planted out in spring at 45cm/18in apart in rows the same distance apart.

BELOW A bed of seakale that will be blanched next winter. To blanch, cover the stems with an upturned bucket or special terracotta pot.

Take root cuttings or thongs from existing plants in autumn. Cut a few side roots that are about 1cm/½in thick into 15cm/6in lengths. Tie these in a bundle and put them vertically (make certain the top of the root is at the top)

in the garden in well-drained soil or in a large pot filled with free-draining compost (soil mix). The top of the roots should be about 5cm/2in below the surface. Towards the end of next spring, once shoots have appeared from

RIGHT Seakale is attractive in flower but once it has reached this stage it is no longer worth harvesting as the stems are no longer blanched.

the bundle, separate them and plant them out at the same intervals as for bought plants. Alternatively, dig up the plants in autumn and place them in boxes of compost with the buds at the surface. Place them in a dark place with the temperature about 10°C/50°F.

Seed should be sown in spring in drills 4cm/1½in deep. Soak the seed in water overnight before sowing. Thin seedlings to 23cm/9in and transplant the resulting seedlings to their final position the following spring.

The stems of seakale can be blanched by covering the plants in late winter or early spring with a special terracotta pot or an upturned bucket. Terracotta pots are more decorative. It is important that no light enters, or the stems will turn green and taste bitter.

BELOW This is a blanched seakale plant that has been exposed to the light once more to grow away again.

HARVESTING

Plants and thongs can be harvested in the second year; those grown from seed in the third year. Harvest when the blanched stems are long enough and remove the covers once harvesting is complete. Discard the plants after harvesting (but remember to take root cuttings when you lift the plants in order to provide the crop for next year).

STORAGE

Eat seakale stems straight from the garden when they are about 20cm/8in long. They will not keep and must be eaten in season only.

PESTS AND DISEASES

On the whole, seakale is trouble free. The worst pests are slugs and caterpillars, especially those of the cabbage white butterfly.

Growing peas

Peas like an open, sunny site. The soil should be fertile, with a pH of 6–6.8, and should have manure or compost incorporated into it during the previous autumn. First earlies can be sown in late autumn and then overwintered; remember to cover the plants with cloches in colder areas. Alternatively, they can be sown in late winter or early spring. They can also be grown under cloches if necessary. Crops can then be sown at intervals until the early summer.

The easiest way to sow peas is to pull out a flat-bottomed trench with a hoe, about 15–20cm/6–8in wide and 5cm/2in deep. The peas are then sown in pairs, one on each side of the trench with the seeds at 5cm/2in intervals. If you

prefer, they can be sown in a single drill at the same intervals. The distance between rows varies from 60 to 90cm (2–3ft), depending on the height of the peas. Add supports when the peas reach

5–8cm/2–3in high and the tendrils start to form. Use plastic pea netting, which is sold specially for the purpose, wire netting or pea-sticks. Once flowering, keep the peas watered during dry weather.

CULTIVATION

Earlies
Sowing time: late autumn, late winter or early spring
Sowing distance: 5cm/2in
Sowing depth: 5cm/2in
Distance between sown rows: 60–90cm/2–3ft
Thinning distance: no need to thin
Harvesting: early summer

Second earlies
Sowing time: early spring
Sowing distance: 5cm/2in
Sowing depth: 5cm/2in

Distance between sown rows: 60–90cm/2–3ft
Thinning distance: no need to thin
Harvesting: early summer

Maincrop
Sowing time: early spring to early summer
Sowing distance: 5cm/2in
Sowing depth: 5cm/2in
Distance between sown rows: 60–90cm/2–3ft
Thinning distance: no need to thin
Harvesting: summer to early autumn

SOWING

Peas can be sown in a double row along a shallow trench, in an open, sunny position.

PROTECTING AGAINST BIRDS

Covering the row with wire netting or fine-mesh nylon netting will prevent birds – especially pigeons – from eating the young seedlings.

ABOVE More than just a small taste of peas can be grown if you use a large container. However, it is important not to let the soil dry out.

ABOVE RIGHT Wire netting can be used to support shorter varieties of peas.

HARVESTING

Pick the pods as soon as the peas have swollen and are large enough to eat. Mangetouts (snow peas) and similar types should be picked before the pods get tough and leathery. Keep picking the peas as they mature. The peas of many modern varieties, which have been created for commercial growers, mature at the same time, and this can be a problem for the gardener.

STORAGE

Peas are best picked straight from the plant, although they can be frozen, which is one way of coping

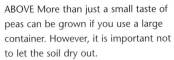

RIGHT Pea-sticks can be used to support tall varieties of peas.

with a glut so that they are available through the whole year. Although it is not common now, they can also be kept by drying.

PESTS AND DISEASES

Unfortunately, peas are prone to quite a number of pests and diseases. At an early stage both mice and birds can eat the seed.

Birds will also strip the emerging seedlings, and it may be necessary to protect them with wire netting. Aphids and pea thrips can also be a problem.

Mildew is something that affects crops most years, especially later in the season. It can be ignored, but you may prefer to use varieties that are less prone to mildew.

Growing runner beans

Beans do best in an open, sunny position; in more exposed areas they should be protected from winds, partly to prevent them from blowing over and partly because pollination is more difficult in such conditions. They will grow in quite poor soil but do best in ground that has been well manured during the previous autumn. They prefer a pH of 6.5. The traditional method is to dig a deep trench and bury plenty of compost and manure, even old newspaper. The idea is not so much to provide nutrients, although this is obviously

important, but to create an area around the roots that retains plenty of moisture.

Runner beans must not appear above ground before the last frost has passed, so early summer is usually the earliest you can begin planting. To get them off to a good start, sow beans individually in pots or modules and plant them out when the weather is right. Alternatively, sow directly into the soil. If you are able to make an early start, it is often a good idea to sow again some three weeks later so that there is a continuous crop until the first frosts of winter.

LEFT A good crop of runner beans with flowers to produce more.

PLANTING

HARVESTING

Runner beans can be planted against a tepee of canes to provide support as they grow. They may need help to start twining up the cane.

1 Harvest the beans when they are large enough, but discard any older, tougher beans. Pick regularly, which may be daily in a good year.

2 Snap or cut the stem just above the bean so that either part of the stalk remains or there is a complete break at the junction between vegetable and stalk.

Before sowing or planting you will need to construct some form of support up which the beans will climb. This can be in the form of a single or double row (double is usually preferable) of poles, canes or strings for them to climb up, or it can be a wigwam or tepee – that is, a circle of poles or canes pulled together at the top with string to form a cone. The distance between the poles or strings should be about 25cm/10in, for although they will grow closer together, it is easier to pick the beans if the plants are not too close.

Plant or sow one bean at each pole. Many gardeners sow two or three beans at each position – "one for the crow, one for the slug and one for the kitchen" – and remove the weaker seedlings, leaving just one. The beans are self-clinging but

may need help to go up the right pole or string, as they often seem to prefer their neighbour's. Make sure that the soil is always moist, especially in dry periods.

Sow or plant dwarf varieties at 15cm/6in intervals in a single row with 45cm/18in between rows. Pinch out any long shoots that develop. After harvesting, cut down the beans but leave the roots to rot in the ground; they contain stores of valuable nitrogen.

HARVESTING

Pick the pods as soon as the beans begin to swell, which is usually when the pods are about 15cm/ 6in long. Some varieties, especially those developed for exhibition, can be considerably longer than this although not necessarily more flavourful. A larger crop can be

encouraged by picking regularly, putting any excess in the freezer. It is also important to pick regularly because old beans become stringy and inedible.

STORAGE

Beans do not keep well and should be eaten as they are harvested. The only storage method used today is freezing, although in the past they were often preserved in salt.

PESTS AND DISEASES

Slugs and snails are always a problem when the plants first emerge, and they can easily kill the entire planting. Runner beans are otherwise generally problem free, apart from possible attacks of blackfly or red spider mite. Powdery mildew and chocolate spot may also occur.

Growing French beans

French (green) beans, both dwarf and climbing, need a sunny, open site. The soil should be fertile but free-draining, preferably manured during the previous autumn. They prefer a neutral soil, with a pH of 6.5–7.5. An early start can be made by sowing the beans in pots or modules under glass in late spring and planting out after the threat of frost has passed. Alternatively, they can be sown directly into the soil and covered with cloches. Most gardeners, however, tend to wait until early summer and sow directly into the soil, when the conditions should be perfect. Sow in a single or double row, spacing the beans about 8cm/3in apart in rows set 45cm/18in apart. They should be

CULTIVATION

Dwarf beans

Sowing time: late spring (under glass) to early summer

Sowing or planting distance: 8cm/3in

Sowing depth: 4cm/1½in

Distance between sown rows: 45cm/18in

Thinning distance: no need to thin

Harvesting: late summer until first frosts

Climbing beans

Sowing time: late spring (under glass) to early summer

Sowing or planting distance: 15–25cm/6–10in

Sowing depth: 4cm/1½in

Distance between sown rows: 90cm/3ft

Thinning distance: no need to thin

Harvesting: late summer until first frosts

planted about 4cm/1½in deep. Climbing or pole varieties should be treated in the same way as runner beans. Keep watered in dry weather.

HARVESTING

Harvesting can usually begin seven or eight weeks after sowing. Pick while the seeds are still immature and go on picking for as long as the beans cook and eat well. Leave those that you want to treat as haricot (navy) beans until the pods have swollen and turned yellow. Cut the whole plants and hang them up in a dry place to complete the drying. Shell and store.

LEFT These climbing French (green) beans are supported by a bamboo cane.

SOWING

Sow the beans outdoors in a single or double trench, once the threat of frosts has passed. Water the trench if the soil is dry and with no prospect of rain.

HARVESTING

Do not to pull too hard when harvesting French beans because the plants may be pulled from the ground. Remove any that have grown too big or tough, to encourage new ones to appear.

STORAGE

French beans are best used fresh from the plant, but they can be frozen, which is a good way of dealing with a glut. Haricot beans should be dried and stored in a dark cupboard in airtight jars.

PESTS AND DISEASES

On the whole French beans are not prone to many problems. Slugs and snails are the most likely nuisance, especially when the plants are first emerging, but they can eat the pods as well.

Blackfly and fungal diseases may also be a problem. Poor crops can result from bad weather deterring pollinating insects.

BELOW These striking purple French beans are now ready for harvesting. It seems a shame to pick such a decorative crop, but on the other hand they are delicious.

Growing broad beans

Broad (fava) beans need an open, sunny site, which is protected from strong winds, especially if you are growing overwintering types. A reasonably fertile soil is required, and this is best achieved by adding manure or compost in the autumn dig. They do best in soil that is on the acid side of neutral with a pH of 6–7. Overwintering varieties can be sown in late autumn. Other types should be sown in late winter or early spring. New varieties have extended the sowing season until early summer, but most need to be sown by the end of spring.

Make sure that early-sown beans get off to a good start by putting cloches over the ground a couple of weeks before you intend to sow. This will warm up the soil. Sow in double rows in a shallow

CULTIVATION

Sowing time: late autumn, late winter to late spring
Sowing or planting distance: 23cm/9in
Sowing depth: 4cm/1½in
Distance between sown rows: 60cm/24in
Thinning distance: no need to thin
Harvesting: early to late summer

trench, 23cm/9in wide and 4cm/1½in deep. Alternatively, sow each seed individually with a pencil or stick. In both cases, the seeds should be about 23cm/9in apart, and the rows should be 60cm/24in

BELOW A row of healthy young broad (fava) beans at an early stage of their growth. Make certain that they are kept weeded and watered during this period.

apart. Seeds can also be raised in pots or modules in late winter under glass and planted out in spring.

Taller varieties will need to be supported with string tied to canes that are set at intervals along each side of the double row. When the beans are in full flower, pinch out the tender top by 8cm/3in to reduce the chance of blackfly infestation and to make the pods fill out. Keep the plants well watered during dry periods.

HARVESTING

Pick the pods when the beans inside them have swollen. Some can be picked at an earlier stage for cooking whole.

Do not allow the beans to become too old – that is, when they are leathery and pliable –

ABOVE Taller varieties of broad beans will need supporting with string tied to canes that are set at intervals along the rows.

RIGHT This row of broad beans is being supported with canes and string.

or they will be tough and too floury. Some people like to cook and eat the young tops.

STORAGE

These beans are undoubtedly best when picked straight from the plant before the pod is leathery, but any excess can be frozen for future use. They can also be dried.

PESTS AND DISEASES

The most serious problem is black-fly, but this can often be avoided by removing the tips of the plant. Mice will dig up and eat the beans.

On the whole, these beans are reasonably trouble free, although chocolate spot can be a problem. This can usually be ignored, but burn or destroy the affected plants when they are finished with, rather than put them on the compost heap. Grey mould will affect plants grown too close together.

PINCHING OUT

Pinching out the tops of the beans is a good practice because it discourages blackfly and encourages even growth. The tops can then be boiled and eaten.

Index

The publisher would like to thank the following for supplying pictures: *Tim Ellerby* 38bl; *Garden Picture Library* 55t; *Garden World Images* 39t, b, 47b, 63r.